What Causes a Rainbow?

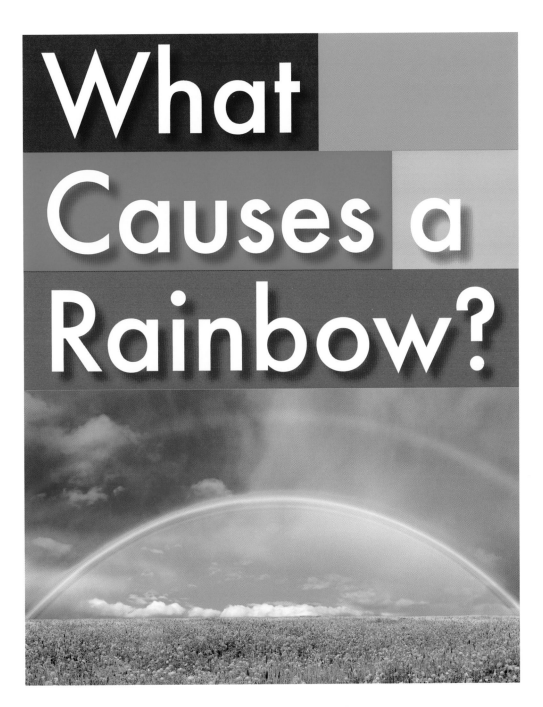

by Janet Slingerland

E
551.567
SLi

childsworld.com

Published by The Child's World®
1980 Lookout Drive • Mankato, MN 56003-1705
800-599-READ • www.childsworld.com

Acknowledgments
The Child's World®: Mary Swensen, Publishing Director
Red Line Editorial: Editorial direction and production
The Design Lab: Design

Photographs ©: Pichugin Dmitry/Shutterstock Images, cover,
1; Tatyana Bond/Shutterstock Images, 5; Roman Samokhin/
Shutterstock Images, 7; Shutterstock Images, 9, 11, 19, 21; Red
Line Editorial, 13; NASA, 15; iStockphoto, 17

ISBN 9781503807914
LCCN 2015958140

Printed in the United States of America
Mankato, MN
June, 2016
PAO2299

ABOUT THE AUTHOR

Janet Slingerland is a writer,
a scout leader, and an engineer.
She loves books, science, and
books about science. She lives
in New Jersey with her husband
and three children.

TABLE of CONTENTS

CHAPTER 1

What Is Light?

Light is energy that moves as a wave. Light waves look like a line of hills. They go up and down. They move very fast. Waves have wavelengths. This is the length from the top of one wave to the top of the next.

Light has three **primary** colors. They are blue, red, and green. These colors of light can mix together to make all other colors. When you mix blue paint with red paint, you make the color violet. The same thing happens with light.

Light waves move up and down.

When blue light and red light are combined, the result is violet light.

But what happens when you mix a bunch of different colors of paint together? The mixed paint turns black or dark brown. Colors of light are different. When all of them are mixed together, the result is not black—it is white! White light from the sun or a lamp does not lack color. It is the mix of all colors of light.

We are able to see six basic colors: red, orange, yellow, green, blue, and violet. We see the three primary colors of light. We see other colors by mixing different colors of light. Red light mixed

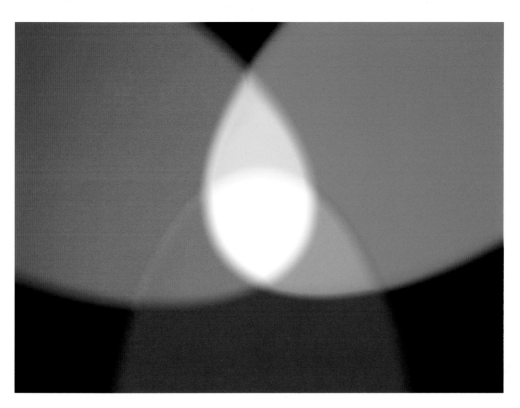

When you shine blue light, red light, and green light on top of one another, you get white light!

with green light looks yellow. Each color of light has a different wavelength. Red light has the longest wavelength. Violet has the shortest. The rest are in between.

CHAPTER 2

What Makes Rainbow Colors?

In a rainbow, we see red, orange, yellow, green, blue, and violet. These rainbow colors come from white light. We can use a prism to break apart white light and see the different colors in it. A prism is shaped like a triangle. You can see through it. Many prisms are made of glass. A prism breaks white light into colors. White light goes in. A rainbow comes out. How does this happen?

Light moves fast in air. It slows down a little bit when it enters a prism.

You can see the white light going into this prism and rainbow colors coming out.

9

This makes the light bend. Some colors of light slow down more than others. This makes them bend more. Violet light bends the most. Red bends the least.

The light bends again when it leaves the prism. Each color bends differently. This breaks them apart more. It makes the colors easier to see.

Water can act as a prism. Light slows down when it enters the water. This makes the light bend. The light bends again when it leaves the water. Each color bends differently. This makes the rainbow colors easy to see.

*The glass and the water bend light. This makes
the stripes behind the glass look backward.*

CHAPTER 3

When Do We See a Rainbow?

Raindrops are in the air just before and just after it rains. A rainbow forms when sunlight enters a raindrop. The water drop acts as a prism. The light bends when it enters each raindrop. Each color bends at a different **angle**. The light now has bands of colors. The bands of color hit the back of the raindrop. The light **reflects** and bends back. Each band of color bends differently. The colors break apart more. The light leaves the raindrop.

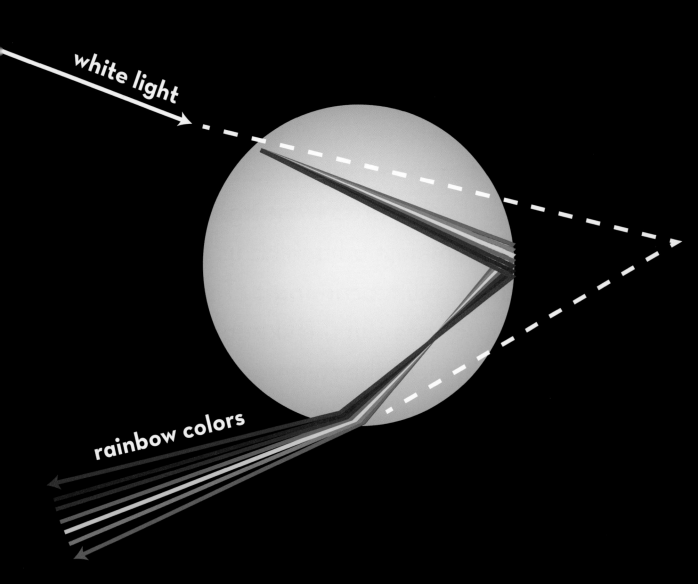

white light

rainbow colors

White light enters a raindrop. It bends and reflects. Rainbow colors leave the raindrop.

The light bends again. Rainbow colors are now **visible** across the sky.

We have to be in the right place to see a rainbow. Rainbow light must reach our eyes for us to see it. White light from the sun enters the raindrop. Rainbow light leaves the raindrop from the same side.

The sun must be behind us. The raindrops must be in front of us. The sun must be low in the sky. If the sun is too high, the rainbow light goes above us. We do not see the rainbow. We must be between the sun and the rain to see rainbows.

*We need the sun behind us and raindrops
in front of us to see a rainbow.*

CHAPTER 4

What Shape Are Rainbows?

We think of rainbows as curves. We picture **arcs** in the sky. But that is only because we do not see the whole rainbow! Rainbows are really circles. The ground blocks our view. We see only part of the circle.

Pilots sometimes see circle rainbows from their airplanes. The rain is below them. They look down through the rain. The ground does not get in the way. So they can see the whole rainbow.

It matters where the sun is, too. We see more of the rainbow when the sun is low.

You can see the whole rainbow if you are high enough in the sky.

We see less when the sun is higher. We do not see it at all if the sun is too high.

There can be more than one rainbow at a time. Light reflects off the backs of raindrops. This makes a primary rainbow. This is the kind of rainbow you often see. The top of this rainbow is red. The bottom is violet.

The light can reflect inside the raindrops one more time. This makes a **double** rainbow, and it is different. The colors are in the opposite order. The top color is violet. The bottom is red.

Did you know you can see a rainbow at night? It does not happen often.

Rainbows can be reflected in lakes or oceans.

There has to be a lot of moonlight. A night when the moon is full is best. The rest of the sky has to be very dark. Then you can see moonlight reflecting off raindrops in the air at night. This is called a moonbow. The colors in a moonbow are not very bright. This is because moonlight is not as strong as sunlight.

The next time it rains, wait for the sun to come out. The raindrops might act as prisms. Make sure the sun is behind you. See if you spy a rainbow. Maybe it will even be a double!

In a double rainbow, the second rainbow is a mirror image of the first.

Make a Water Prism

You just learned about what causes a rainbow. Now try to reflect light on your own!

What You Need
round, clear glass or jar
water
flashlight (not LED)
white paper

What to Do
1. Make sure the glass or jar is clean. Fill it half full of water. Set the glass on the white paper.
2. Darken the room. Turn on the flashlight. Hold the flashlight at an angle. Point it at the water.
3. Look at the light coming out of the glass. Slowly move the flashlight around. Look for rainbow colors. Look at the edges of the light. The rainbow colors may be there.
4. The glass and water act as a prism. They separate the light into rainbow colors.

Glossary

angle (ANG-guhl) An angle is the point where two lines meet. A triangle has three angles.

arcs (ahrks) Arcs are curved lines. We imagine rainbows as arcs.

double (DUHB-uhl) An object is double when there are two of them. A double rainbow has two rainbows together.

primary (PRY-mayr-ee) Primary colors are the set of colors that all other colors are made from. Blue, green, and red are the primary colors of light.

reflects (ri-FLEKTS) Light reflects when it bounces off an object. Light reflects off water.

visible (VIZ-uh-buhl) An object is visible when we can see it. Visible light is light we can see.

To Learn More

In the Library

Beaton, Kathryn. *I See Rainbows (Tell Me Why?)*.
Ann Arbor, MI: Cherry Lake, 2015.

Coan, Sharon. *Light Makes a Rainbow*.
Huntington Beach, CA: Teacher Created Materials,
2014.

Rajczak, Kristen. *Rainbows (Nature's Light Show)*.
New York: Gareth Stevens, 2012.

On the Web

Visit our Web site for links about how rainbows work:
childsworld.com/links

*Note to Parents, Teachers, and Librarians: We routinely verify our Web links to make sure
they are safe and active sites. So encourage your readers to check them out!*

Index